AF372292

Ethereal

Dreamlands and Heavens

-Second Edition-

Bryce Couture

Also by Bryce Couture

Fur and The Finer Things

Sea of Life

Lovely Lovers

Dedications

Kellianne Philips -
the poem "Something About Galaxies"

Brianna Sears -
the poem "Elvis"

My Mother
the poem "Heaven is Real"

My Mammy
the poem "Green Thumb"

Ethereal

Dreamlands and Heavens

Ethereal -

extremely delicate and light in a way that seems too perfect for this world.

Oasis

Let's go to oasis
with velvet skies and birds who fly
bumble bees and willows trees
can you imagine?
all the wonder you can imagine

I can't think of a better place
bliss and essence free
take a trip and feel the glee
to oasis

Let us travel with the crows
while the winds heavy blow
can you imagine?
all the life you imagine

Where raindrops cry
and the wind is alive
take a trip to oasis
travel onto the sky

Cadillac

Take me to Hotel Bonaventure Montreal
buy me roses and love
take me out and take me down
spin my head all around
there's pieces of me lost in you
you say you love my eyes
and my attitude
you call me Cadillac
better than the rest before
you tattooed my name on your soul
take me to the shore
dance with me in the moonlight
I tell you to take it off
buy me love and get me drunk
i'm your midnight fighter
so take me away and let's stay
the air flows between us
our palms touch
he calls me cocaine
addictive and pure
tells me i'm forever young
but destructive to touch
he loves the way I say his name
tells me everyday

I will follow you into the dark
forever young
Cadillac

Flower Amore

Light of the night
I want you, I need you
petals and leaves
dark of despair
I crave you, all of you
roots vengeance
I let you, I am you
breathe life
amore

Rain

I wilted while waiting for you
my jungles collapsed
my leaves turned brown
and my vines were no longer divine

Rain pour, galore

I cried while it rained without you
my tropics drowned
my roots just rotted
and my flowers will not tower

Rain shower, blood flower

Garden Party

I want my head between your thighs
all the stars are in your eyes
hibiscus and velvet
with Rick Nelson
the garden party plays
you are in a haze
flowers and whiskey
he wants to kiss me
this heaven is bliss
while we french kiss

Calypso

My dearest calypso
she comes from the sea
her mind like a diamond
always coming for me

My haunting mistress
she is ultimately free
her soul is damned
darling come to me

My dark damsel
she holds the church key
her body magnificent
staring at me

My bloody duchess
she is gutsy
her voice is luring
drawing me

Come Home Soon

I was thinking
about the bees, the sky
and how i wanted you to be mine
I started to realize everything
I did wrong or right
how I could've done better
how it could've turned out better
but i'm content with how it did
my life is mine and only mine
every failure is my success
to achieve greatness in the stars
so when I said I wanted you
I didn't mean now or later
but a promise that someday
I could hold you under the light
of the heavens and breathe
because you are the greatness
I want to obtain
in the glass jar on my shelf
you are the soul I want to touch
I don't care how many you've been with
or how many you will leave me for

as long as I know I am the one
that you come home to
when you're scared and weak
grasping onto life
I will hold you and fix you
make you better and bright
and I watch you walk out that door
I will smile for you are mine
in the end for all eternity
come home soon

Ethereal

Green meadows with roses
and a tangerine colored sky
the water sparkling with bliss
as I watch the clouds pass by
the birds, they call from above
harmonizing a heavenly hymn
there is no time, only peace
the swans of gold swim

The warmth of human embrace
not a single flower petal will fall
only dreams are reality
the garden, a masquerade ball
come take my hand and walk
let us kiss under the peach tree
our hearts sing and souls revel
then we are ethereal and eternally free

The Jungle

In the jungle of blood and desire
lust fills your veins
controls your mind
breaks your heart

The flowers of passion will arise
vines of truth will choke
you must run
you must hide

Protect yourself from these
they will be your downfall
you must live

Give yourself over to absolute pleasure
lose yourself in the essence
gain immortality
for a short time

How does it feel?
to be divine
to be alive

How does it taste?
the sweat and the tears
sweet bliss

So tell me little harpy
what do you see when you soar
the jungle below so small
do you smell the blood?

With your talons around there neck
they will feel alive
free from sin

Does she free you from your prison?
make you taste the light

Give yourself over to her
she is your master
it is her whom controls the night
orders the darkness

There is no escaping the jungle of blood and desire
for it consumes you internally
you are trapped
for eternity

Oh sweet wyvern
guide them to the jungle
teach them how to sing

majestic and free
breathing lust's fire
leading the stray

Your body so elegant
and heart so true

He will make you taste the wind
let go of your soul
he will care for you
mend you

Oh solemn manticore
you lack in passion
filled with hate and distrust

Rough and wild
still drawing a crowd

He will cut you open
watch you bleed
destroy you

But you will let him
you will laugh and cry
beg for more

In the jungle of blood and desire
the harpy will fly
with grace and beauty
the wyvern will lead you
to passion and freedom
the manticore will destroy you
and make you beg for more

It is worth the journey
don't be coy

For if you enter the jungle of blood and desire
all of your darkest fears and fantasies
will intertwine and breathe life
into your hollow soul

Wretched are those who leave
free are those who die
tormented are those who refuse

Joy

Can I touch the sand
or hold your hand
up in the sky in heaven
fantasy land and strawberry pie
I see yellows and golds
I have a warm fuzzy feeling
a glow around the palm trees
riches and golds don't matter there
there is light that surrounds us
joy takes over us
I want my hand in your hand
and your thighs belong to me
come up to fantasy land
once upon a dream
you will see

Dreamland

Don't let my tears mistake you
this is wonderland
happy pills and hundred dollar bills
dancing at night to old tunes
swaying with the wind
pretty face and perky smile
this is the happy place
trailer parks and stretch marks
kissing anyone and everyone
laughing all night
empty emotions
this is my dreamland
insanity and profanity

Ocean Blvd.

*This place is not my home
my home is the open road
Ocean Blvd. and the sunset view
fireworks and cigarettes
my home is with the ones I love
even if they do not love me
these things don't matter
the sky consumes me
the tar and the paint
but my home is where I choose
no residency
manor or estate
my home is with myself alone
the sea is my home
the flowers and the birds
she welcomes me
but my home travels
no set point
in life I have a home
constant and free*

Celestial

I died everyday while waiting for you
now I am in ethereal
my dreams and my reality
void of all emotion
do not leave my mind
the presence of you is irreplaceable
I have made up what you smell like
what your touch or gaze feels like
or how it would be
if you loved me
I adore you more than life itself
so I gave it up
I let it all go just to spend eternity with you
in my head of games and sorrow
I breathe the celestial now
but yearn to touch you
all of the stars and wealth onto me
could I trade for you

It is not so bad here
illusion and false butterflies
but I get the vision of you
forever I could look upon you

only my life for you
I can not touch or feel
always out of reach
tricking your eyes but not your soul
I know it is not you and never will be
but in that moment I feel infinite
because I feel it could be
I feel it could be you

At the Swimming Pool

They laid there
tanning and waiting
sun hats and white sunglasses
one-piece but heart split in two
rippling waves and soft skies
the sun kissed them
bright lipstick and wishes
waiting for henry
oh honey, oh henry
oh sparkling bliss
heavenly peace
swimming pools
and shade trees
yellow, pink, blue too
oh henry, oh baby
money in the air
a kiss on the cheek too
but come and dance
heavenly blues

Numb

Just the thought of your voice
makes my soul come undone
with every echo of you
my body becomes numb

Your breathe is morning dew
and your tears of holy water
shivers down my spine
I am a cut and you are saltwater

Those eyes of passion
that sharp chin of lust
brings me to my knees
and my mind to dust

With every waking hour
and you not by my side
I become hollow
while watching high tide

Stay

Rain storms and rain clouds
only pour away
the heart and the soul
of the one you touch
each and every day
you sit and ponder
he likes to play
take my hand
a dip in the bay
with every waking moment
you love him today
with the rush of tears
you kneel down and pray

Something About Galaxies

The stars in the sky
after a violet disaster
the tears of a mermaid
metamorphosis after

I Found the One

A love greater than the stars
not even Marilyn could deny
a touch of heaven and hollywood
enough to even make her cry
tears of jewels on porcelain skin
I think they are the one
you are the moon and all the stars
the light of my rising sun

Midnight Drive

Maybe it's the tunnel lights
or the little pieces of you,
that I find in the night
either way this is heaven
in darkness there is white

Le Diable

The devil does not have horns or red skin
but he does have killer eyes
and a touch so good to make you sin

I never sold my soul, but he stole my heart
everything he does flows like a rhyme
you won't even know you're falling apart

Rose

While trying to pick a petal
I bleed from a thorn
even with the velvet grove
she is still forlorn
with every passing stranger
she is left to mourn
her tears feed the garden
lush blossoms reborn

Dream

Life's true pleasures are seen
only behind the closed eyes of a dream
all of the shadows will gleam
and soft ice cream
where you do not need self esteem
the freeness and beauty to scream
smiles and whipped cream

Elvis

Elvis the pelvis
with blue suede shoes in hand
take a walk on the beach
with our toes in the sand
dreamy eyes and voice up on a cloud
with the roars and the rumbles
the screams of an adoring crowd

Elvis please come get hellish
I can't help falling in love
the music you play is so charming
my soul soars like a mourning dove
you take me to another space
a whole new world, existence
an experience I couldn't replace

Paradise

I love this place and the absence of logic
the ideas it brings me and the peace it has
from the sea and the shore
to the garden with hydrangea
this is the life I am creating
the clocks run forever
day and night fused together as one
the faint sound of orchestras far away
there is no harm in dreaming
eyes of the eternal look into my soul
maybe this place is crazy and unreal
or maybe just insane enough to be real
either way smell the air
let the water rush over you
and your soul dive into paradise

Dear Future Lover

The thought that someone could love me
makes my knees weak
do you wish upon the stars like me?
the same exact ones
we are strangers and could be for a while
you could be on the other side of the world
with dreams and thoughts of things
that I would never even imagine
are your eyes blue? or maybe brown?
your hair curly or straight
all I know is that I have a hollow spot
like a puzzle missing a piece
that the idea of a soulmate could fill
I will patch up your holes as well
we can hold each other up
like two rotting trees
I have you
and you have me

Serendipity

The way the record spins
or how the cigarette burns
makes me feel nostalgic

Maybe warm coffee
or listening to the tide against the rocks
is what makes me feel alive

The thought that we are all going to die
or all the sleepless nights
makes me carefree

Maybe a pen stroke on paper or beautiful art
is what makes me feel satisfied
but in-between the madness
a fortune stroke of serendipity

Heaven is Real

Have you ever sat and watched the tide
or listened to the birds sing?
maybe you have walked barefoot on grass
or watched your mother laugh?
you have to watch the sunrise with the
people that you love, hold them close
you must dance and feel your heartbeat

I know when I look at the sky
or watch the waves pass by
that life has no end
and is a dear friend
for heaven is on earth
all around us everyday, open your eyes
Heaven is real
and it is a color wheel

Sangria Sunset

With a warm fuzzy feeling
green eyes with a sparkle
we drink wine and ginger ale
the music plays
and our toes touch the cold floor
everything is spinning and a buzz
laughing so hard we cry
touching me, touching you
when the sun rises again
riesling morning dew
a summer mist
you dance for me
while I watch you

Oceans Demons

With the perfect mix
of rebellion and power
oceans choir sing to me
gorillas on silver chains
jewels line the beaches
the sunset dancing like koi
what are your thoughts on this eternity?
can you be in love with a place
or maybe just a pretty face
nevermind just listen
the orchestral demons sing
the song of spring

Bliss

Everything was dark that day
than the sky came to play
purple fog dropped from the heavens
the glamour of gods

The air was thick and colorful
my heart was lustful
as the sky turned pink
and the light filled the horizon

Blue grass and maroon trees
fruit so bountiful
what is this place?
what is this peace?

Everything grew bright that day
perfection as you would say
every color in the morning dew
every piece of bliss with you

Orange and Blue

Hibiscus are orange
hydrangeas are blue
all flowers wither
just like my love for you

Into the Rose Garden

Some people trust their life
in the smile of a loved one
who holds a knife

So you must flea and you must leave
find freedom in rushing water
and beauty in the atmosphere

But now they fear of dreaming
recollection of events
misfortune they are redeeming

When you cannot escape in thoughts
and memories haunt your soul
climb the shrubs and fall into ecstasy

Because the ones you love the most
will destroy your mind
only to leave and become a ghost

Infatuation

Temptation of the body
song of the mind
soft melodies
lips so kind

Infatuation of the soul
wine made from sweat
luscious roses
eyes like the sunset

Breathe me, feel me

We're Jaded

My head up in the clouds
as I watch the time pass by
color swirls and light dances
the cranes, up high they fly

Everything is so beautiful
from the ocean to the sky
every piece of life created
even you cannot deny

As I linger on the past
sometimes we all have to cry
we bathe in hot water
jaded, we drip-dry

Vinyl

You make my heart spin
lavender and blue
a haze or a trance
my kinda music too

Maybe we could talk for hours
mr born to be my baby blue
a spectacular turn of events
looking at me as I look at you

Turn up and get down
i've been feeling sad and blue
longing for heartbreak
you'll be stuck on me like glue

Melatonin

Take a little pretty pill
sleepless nights no more
swallow it with rose water
you have nothing to cry for

Consume me in dreams
take me to the sky
take me to cremeland
take magic and bye-bye

Bring me to the ocean
let me walk the shore
white flower petals
rock me to my core

Let me watch the clouds
splash water on the leaves
listen to them sing
our dreams as thick as thieves

Escape is such a wrong word
the canaries they soar
white with light
the entrance a french door

Rejuvenating

I like the silver chain around your neck
the little things about your body
the moles and the creases
give me a little bawdy

The way you hold yourself
makes the cherubs on the ceiling blush
you are so rejuvenating
all of this gives me a rush

With your dark hair and green eyes
you make my spirit soar
you could stay here a little longer
another drink i'll pour

Moonlight

Would you like to dance
nude in the moonlight
listen to the night creatures
my fingers on your waist
your body against mine
our souls intertwined
like the vines overgrown
in the garden nearby
toes on the grass
our eyes like nightlights
brighter than the star-studded sky
as our lips touch
the sky goes white
shooting stars and asteroids
ours spirits and our bodies
we are the night dancers
midnight prancers
nude in the moonlight

Holy Days

The incense burns
reminds me of church
thoughts about god
the blessed mother mary
and sin
if I came to your golden gates
would you let me in
forgive all my mistakes
I have created my version of heaven
inside my own head
I haven't seen much of you
but I have felt you near
the devil has haunted me
can you cast him away
does not believing in the bible
have to mean I don't believe in you
because I do, I do, I do
heavenly father forgive me my sins
bless me in the name
of the father
the son
and the holy spirit
amen

Melody

Go and play your symphonies
touch me like a melody
let the harps play
violins and cellos
go and play the orchestra
but touch me like a melody
they say, they say
you can't play the songs
go bring the beat
bring the heat
and touch me like the melodies

Come Find Me

Baby come find me
i'm in the pink fields
i'm lost, come find me
I want to live in the Chateau Marmont
come find me
the petals on my skin
looking over my shoulder at you
with the only youth I will ever have
glitter and dust rise up
sleepless daydreams
darling come find me
i'm by the purple meadow
i'm never found, come find me
I want to live inside of a star
come find me
refreshing air
breathe in, and out
now run
come find me

In Love With the Sky

Sometimes I wonder
what it would be like to live
behind a waterfall
or at the bottom of the sea
is heaven really on top of white clouds
with golden gates and glowing light
or maybe it is just you and me

How do you define what love is
or if you have found your first love
is love even real
maybe love is measured
in the amount of heartbreak that follows
or maybe you can count the butterflies
to see if they add up to enough
sometimes I feel to much
sometimes to little

Do you ever
walk around and look at the world
and realize the beauty in it
almost like opening your eyes
for the first time

or do you ever
drag yourself around the house
staring out the windows
into space wondering
what everything means

What does it all mean though
why are we here
and how do we know to breathe
without thinking
are bumble bees in love with flowers
do they see the beauty in one
like we do
bees get up close and personal
a microscope to beauty
how does one measure beauty?
by the colors possibly

I think all of this as I sit and wonder why
and how you have made me feel this way
that the stars and the universe
look a bit duller without you
what is this poison
you have put into my veins
to make me infatuated by you

I'm not sure if I love you or the idea of you
or maybe because you were the first
to take my breath away

I wonder if a pointy flower has ever pricked
a bee and caused it pain
would they try to come back for more
or do they learn from the pain
I have not

So do you think living behind a waterfall
would be enchanting
water has never broken a heart
maybe a neck or two
but never a heart
I can picture a rainbow on the other side

The sun loves the moon
and the stars love the sky
but none of them had problems
like you and I
so here we are laughing at our old jokes
but this is the last time
we must say goodbye

Do you think if I climbed the mountains
I could reach the sky?
because i've seen all the wonder in the world
and I want something more
something high
when I look to the clouds
I realize everything now

I was never in love with you or the flowers
I was in love with the sky
I spent hours talking to the stars
and smiling at the moon
when we fought I would cry to the night sky
when we laughed I would jump
towards the sunlight
I never loved you I just thought I did
you could never keep my attention
just a distraction

I know someday when my body
is broken and gone
my soul will join the stars
up high in the night sky
if you ever feel lonely don't look up
for the canvas will go dark

Because you were always second place
and I will not comfort you if you try
because I never loved you
i've been in love with the sky

Sleeping With Flowers

Sleeping is easy when you're
surrounded by flowers
the pansies sing the song of slumber
the petunias count the sheep
the leaves as your linens
the petals are deep

Lay your head
fall into a deep coma
and lucid dreams
in the morning
morning dew aroma

The cherry blossoms will fall
covering you
awake and rise
rested and tall
because you sleep better
surrounded by a flower wall

Everything is Blue

All of this sadness is bad for my skin
but everything is blue
blue hue and diamonds
stargazer, celestial watcher
close the curtains
let down the blinds
we are immortal here
we can never leave

Feeling empty inside
let's lay in the night sky
like a float in water
looking into nothing
tears filling our hollow souls
everything is blue
dark hue and lions

Land of Devils and Gods

Heaven and hell
come together as one
in my head
in this place
in the land of ethereal
a mix of holy and sin
watch the angels and demons sing
harmony of yin and yang
from the garden
to the celestial
this place is a dream
look at anything
you can see light and dark
everything is grey and colorful
in this place
my home
land of devils and gods

Green Thumb

I loved plants and flowers so much
but they always died
I never thought taking pictures
could keep them always alive

Now they are on paper
I have the ink black thumb
the droplets on the petals
last forever and are never done

Leaves transform to lovers
a thorn writing on paper
the room filled and thick
my poems water vapor

Lovebirds

The smell of cologne lingers in the air
with a rush of rage and youth
in that moment under the lights
I feel infinite and freedom sets in
this feels like Florida again
this time with you
puffing the cigarette
puffing our hearts
can we be lovebirds
lost without one another
singing songs of sweet pure love
as the lights go passing above
one, two and three
i hum a song that reminds me of you
we will never be this pretty
we will never be this young
but when the lovebird's sing
that all vanishes and goes away
your song makes my spirit flutter
flap our wings and fly
let's go to Silver Springs
with cologne and youth
our lovebirds fly

Blue Fox

Red is the color of passion
that is why I stuck to blue
even after lustful nights
I made my way back to you

Blue sticks around
red crumbles fast
because everyone knows
blue will always last

Passion is nice for the evening
but eventually fades and goes away
but in the night driving home
I know you will stay

You were my favorite color
even though I had the whole box
anything I wanted to choose from
but you were my blue fox

Ethereal Finale

Into the dreamland and unto the sky. false realities and butterflies, red skies above the glistening water with swans of gold elegant and free passing by in my ethereal heaven. Peach trees and a masquerade of flowers towering high above the horizon. Take my hand and let us travel through the mango colored fields and the life we could have, the life we should have had.

Hold the roses, pray for us and come to the celestial to sin with us. Dance at night to heavenly blues and look me in the eye when you are talking. Jazz and soft grunge taking the night with the help of the birds and the souls of mankind.

With the tears of my people and your heart in hand, jump in the bay and stay for the day and everything might just be okay. I know that everything seems so surreal and might have you thinking that it is all an illusion or some drug trip but I assure you it is real, just reach out and touch it all, reach out and grasp life.

This is what heaven looks like it, feels like and smells like. Everything of your own design and unique, inside the mind and possibly the soul. Here there is no time or space, if you close your eyes you can see the ghosts of your past walk through and around you. As we walk through the meadow with your hopes and fears side by side facing us like soldiers at war, because there is a constant war inside our minds of what is good and what is bad, somehow everything always lands in the gray area.

This could all be just a bad dream, just a sad dream, but who knows what is real anymore. even if I touch your face, are you really there?. Do you hear the cellos and violins calling us like children for dinner, we do not want to be late. The swans call and the roses fall, to us and for us to return. We must not question this place and just accept the peace. We must accept that there are not answers for everything, take a dip in the pool and be consumed by daydreams and fantasies.

Index